It's FUNdamental!

Hidden Pictures

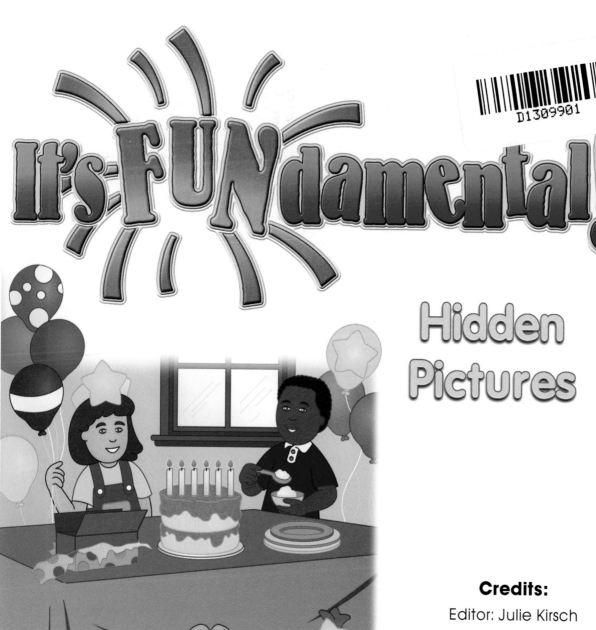

Credits:

Editor: Julie Kirsch

Layout Design: James Cooley

Cover Design and Illustration:

Lori Jackson

ISBN: 978-1-6009-5267-8

Table of Contents

EASY

Reading Rabbits 3
Popcorn Pals....................4
Time for Breakfast 5
Darling Dinosaurs................6
Balloon 7
Frankie Frog 8
Sweet Heart 9
Lovely Leaf.......................10
Alex Alligator 11
Miles of Smiles..................12
Shine On 13
Book Fun 14
Time for a Swim................15
Fire Hydrant.....................16
Having a Ball 17
Olivia Octopus 18
Birthday Star 19
Herbert Hippo 20
Campfire Cookout 21
Cool Carrot......................22
Fancy Flower 23
Under the Sea 24
Tasty Treat.......................25
Bright Idea 26
Tommy Turtle 27
Colorful Candle..................28
Super Slice 29
Benny the Bear 30
Flying High 31
Friendly Skies 32
Wrap It Up........................33

MEDIUM

Sammy Scarecrow............34
Play Ball...........................35
Ski Scene 36
Smooth Sailing..................37
Barnyard Buddies 38
Madison's Room 39
Head of the Class.............40
Grocery Shopping.............41
A Hopping Good Time 42
Out of This World 43
Piece of Cake 44
Cactus 45
A Ducky Day 46
Unlock the Puzzle 47
Super Stars......................48
Colorful Crayons...............49
Percy Pig 50
Ring the Bell 51
Pick of the Patch 52
Acorn..............................53
Going Bananas.................54
Football Fun.....................55
Marvelous Mug 56
Watermelon 57
Bright Bird 58
All Wrapped Up 59
Ice Cream Sundae............60
Space Adventure 61
Yummy Treat 62
An Apple a Day 63
Little Dinosaur 64
Riding the Bus..................65

Best of the Bunch.............66
Seashell 67
Ring-a-Ling 68

HARD

Big Cheese 69
Science Scene..................70
Cool Classroom 71
Bryan's Picnic 72
Sea Scene 73
Curious Camper 74
Library Fun 75
Clarence the Clown 76
Winter Wonder..................77
Happy Bird 78
Scrub-a-Dub 79
Sue's Sand Castle.............80
Jill's Garden 81
Party Pizazz.....................82
A Day at the Beach...........83
Lots of Light 84
Up, Up, and Away 85
Over the Rainbow 86
Simon Snail 87
Setting Sail 88
Cupcake 89
Having a Ball 90
Dandy Drum 91
All Aboard 92
Betsy Butterfly 93
Cheery Cardinal................94
Gumball Machine..............95
From A–Z..........................96

Reading Rabbits

Find this object in the picture. Circle it.

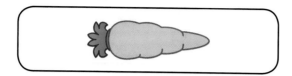

© Rainbow Bridge Publishing

It's FUNdamental! Hidden Pictures

Find this object in the picture. Circle it.

Time for Breakfast

Find these two objects in the picture. Circle them.

It's FUNdamental! Hidden Pictures

5

Find these two objects in the picture. Circle them.

Balloon

Color to find the hidden picture. Color the spaces with circles red. Color the spaces with triangles blue.

⬤ = red   ▲ = blue

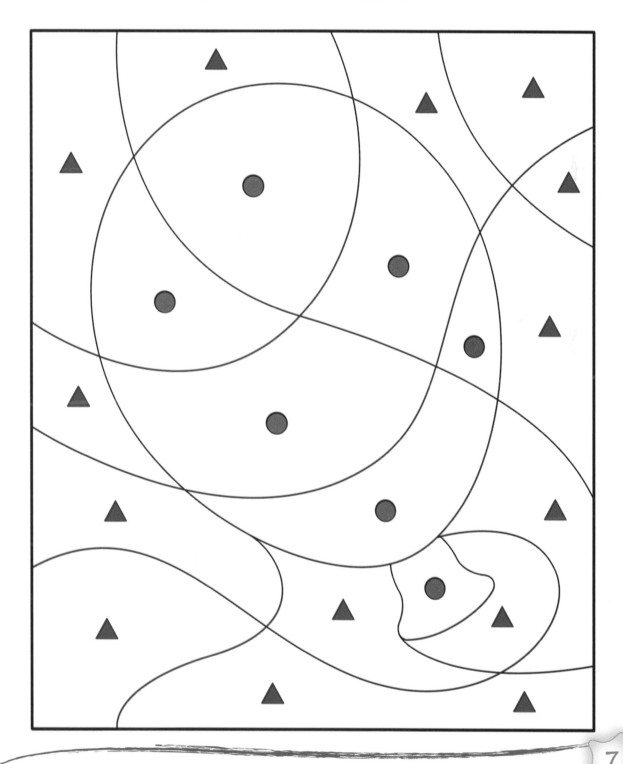

Color to find the hidden picture. Color the spaces with circles green. Color the spaces with squares blue.

● = green   ■ = blue

It's FUNdamental! Hidden Pictures

Sweet Heart

Color to find the hidden picture. Color the spaces with diamonds red. Color the spaces with circles blue.

◯ = blue   ◆ = red

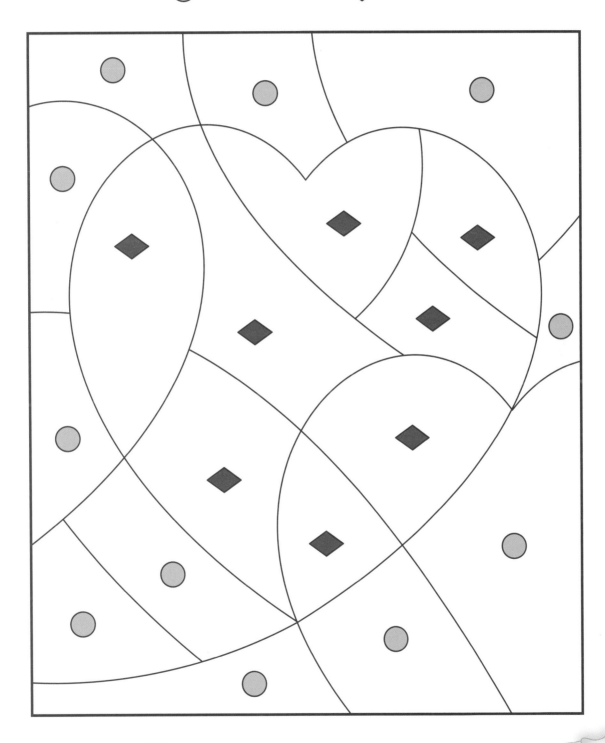

Color to find the hidden picture. Color the spaces with circles orange. Color the spaces with rectangles blue.

⬤ = orange   ▭ = blue

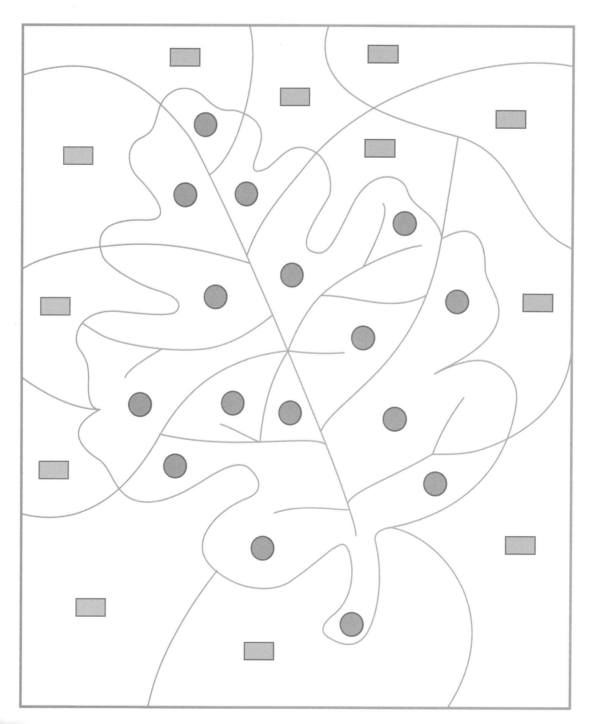

It's FUNdamental! Hidden Pictures

Alex Alligator

Color to find the hidden picture. Color the spaces with ovals green. Color the spaces with circles blue.

⬤ = blue   ⬭ = green

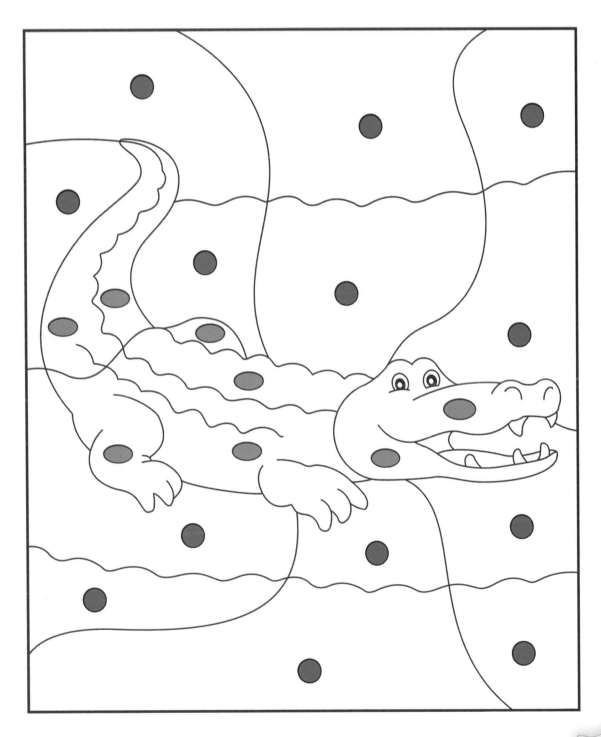

Miles of Smiles

Color to find the hidden picture. Color the spaces with circles green. Color the spaces with triangles purple.

⬤ = green   ▲ = purple

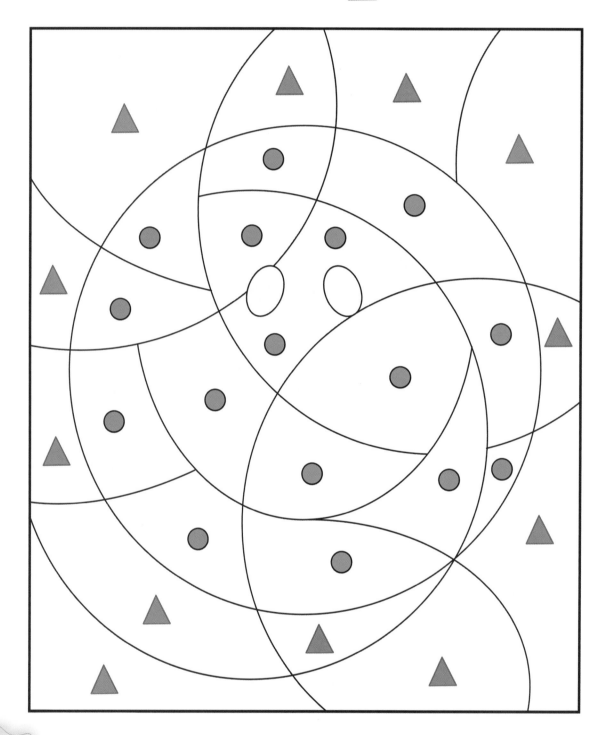

Shine On

Color to find the hidden picture. Color the spaces with triangles yellow. Color the spaces with diamonds blue.

△ = yellow ◇ = blue

It's FUNdamental! Hidden Pictures

Easy

Color to find the hidden picture. Color the spaces with triangles blue. Color the spaces with rectangles green.

▲ = blue   ▬ = green

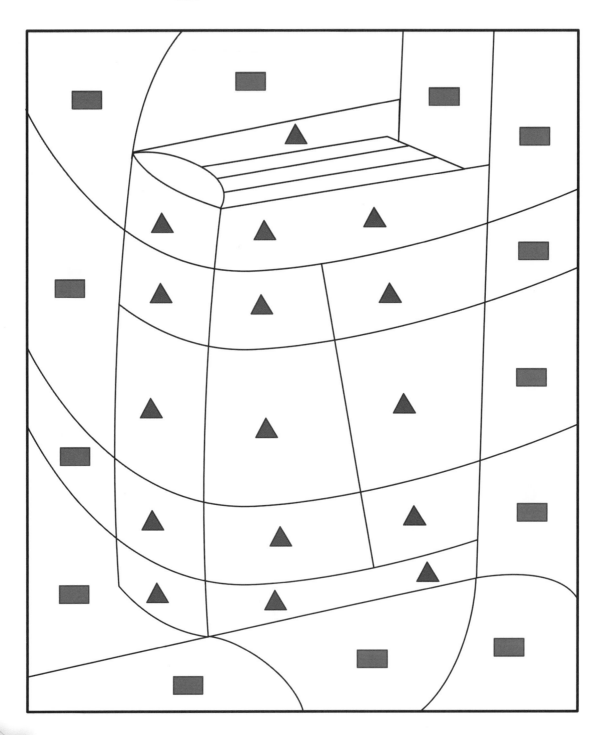

It's FUNdamental! Hidden Pictures

Time for a Swim

Color to find the hidden picture. Color the spaces with ovals gray. Color the spaces with triangles blue.

⬭ = gray　　▲ = blue

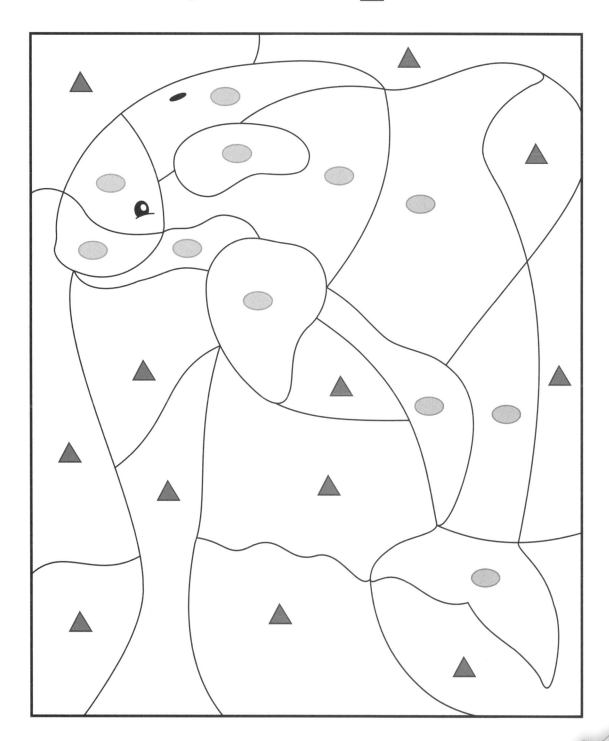

It's FUNdamental! Hidden Pictures

Fire Hydrant

Color to find the hidden picture. Color the spaces with diamonds red. Color the spaces with squares gray.

◆ = red   ▢ = gray

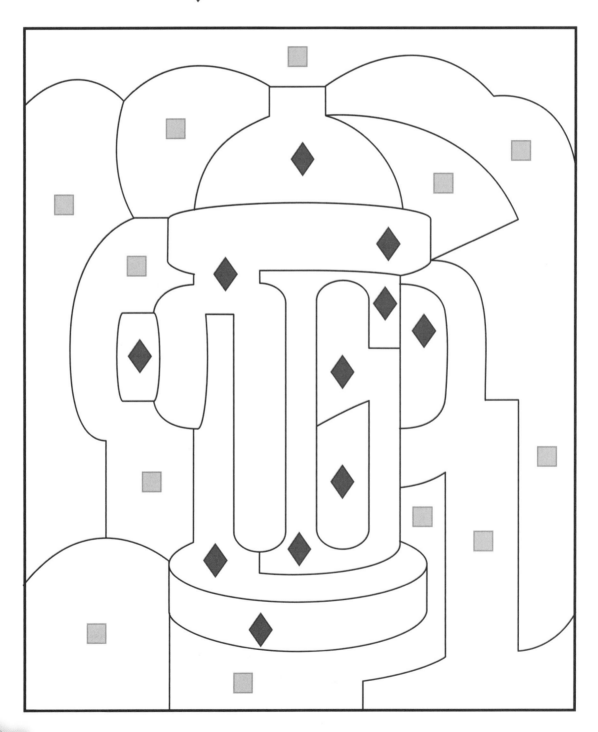

It's **FUN**damental! Hidden Pictures

© Rainbow Bridge Publishing

Having a Ball

Color to find the hidden object. Color the spaces with squares black. Color the spaces with rectangles green.

■ = black   ▬ = green

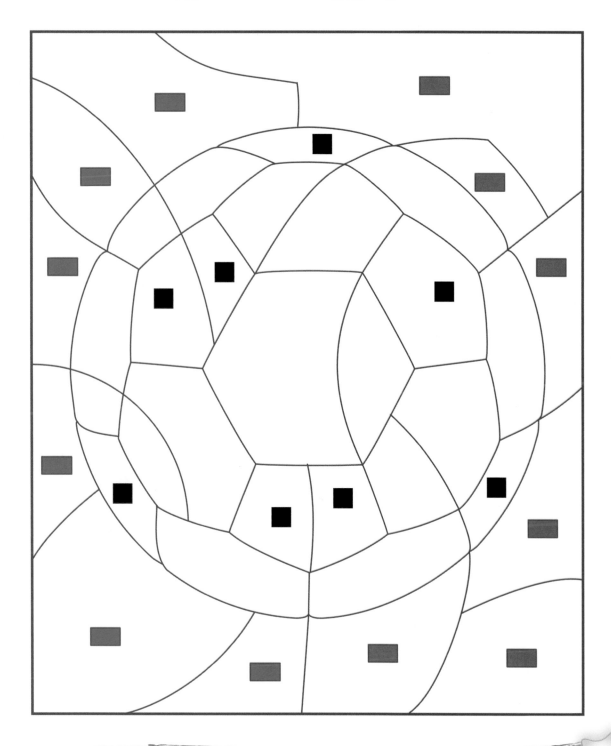

It's FUNdamental! Hidden Pictures

Olivia Octopus

Color to find the hidden picture. Color the spaces with squares pink. Color the spaces with ovals blue.

☐ = pink   ⬭ = blue

It's FUNdamental! Hidden Pictures

Birthday Star

Easy

Find three stars in the picture. Circle them.

© Rainbow Bridge Publishing

It's FUNdamental! Hidden Pictures

19

Find three squares in the picture. Circle them.

Campfire Cookout

Find these three objects in the picture. Circle them.

It's **FUN**damental! Hidden Pictures

Cool Carrot

Color to find the hidden picture. Color the spaces with A's orange. Color the spaces with B's green. Color the spaces with C's blue.

A = orange   **B** = green   **C** = blue

Fancy Flower

Color to find the hidden picture. Color the spaces with B's green. Color the spaces with C's pink. Color the spaces with D's blue.

B = green   **C** = pink   **D** = blue

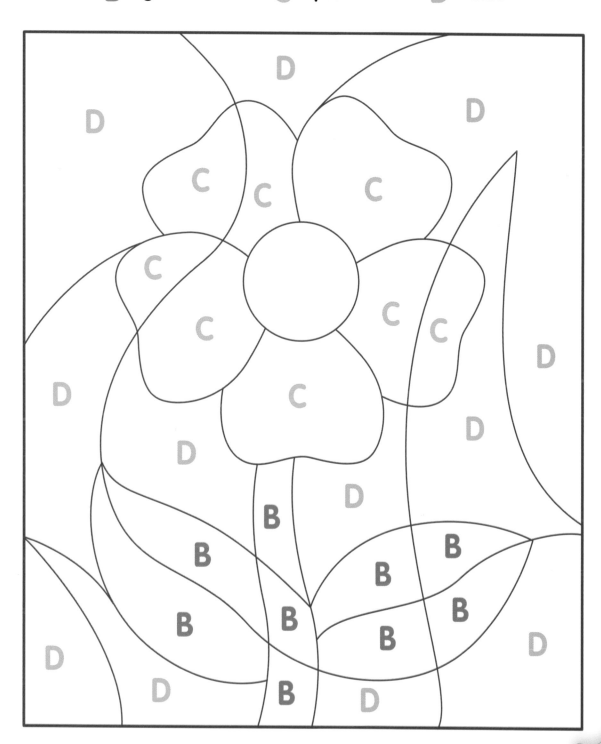

Color to find the hidden picture. Color the spaces with circles yellow. Color the spaces with triangles blue. Color the spaces with squares orange.

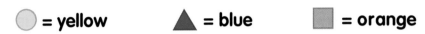

○ = yellow ▲ = blue ■ = orange

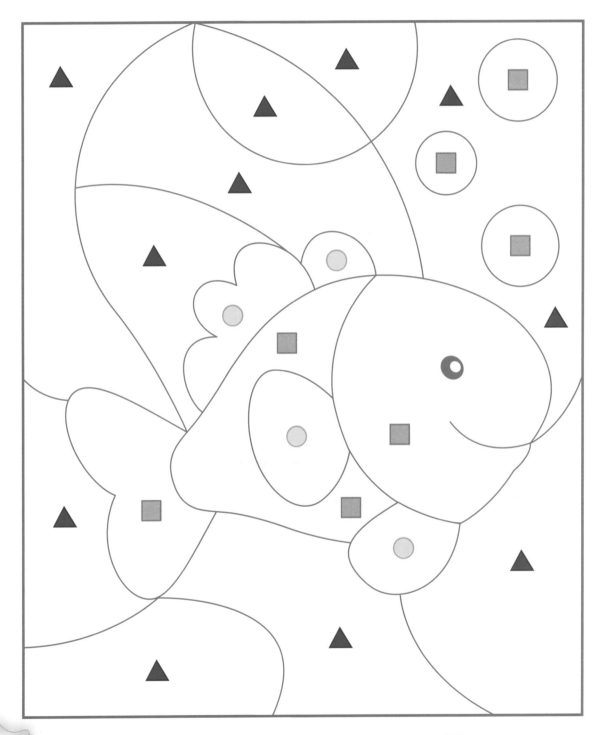

It's FUNdamental! Hidden Pictures

Tasty Treat

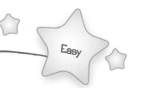

Color to find the hidden picture. Color the spaces with D's brown. Color the spaces with E's yellow. Color the spaces with F's blue.

D = brown   **E** = yellow   **F** = blue

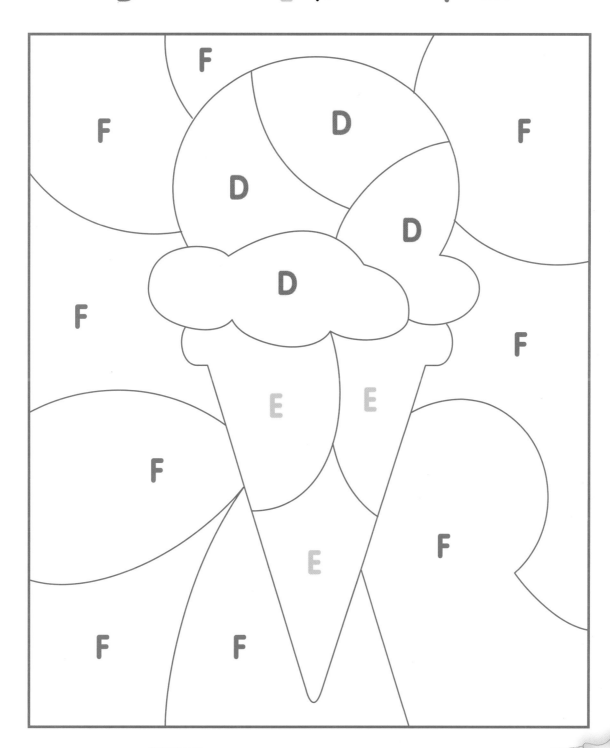

It's FUNdamental! Hidden Pictures

Color to find the hidden picture. Color the spaces with E's yellow. Color the spaces with F's gray. Color the spaces with G's purple.

E = yellow   F = gray   G = purple

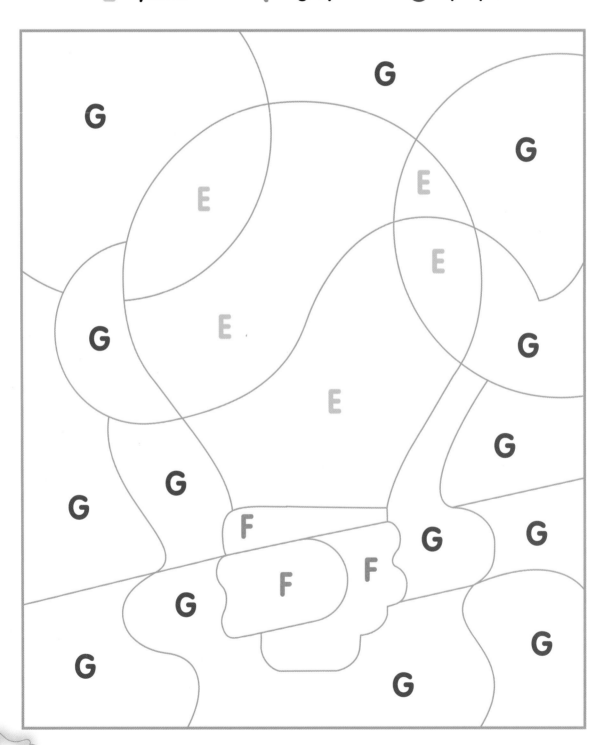

It's FUNdamental! Hidden Pictures

Tommy Turtle

Color to find the hidden picture. Color the spaces with F's green. Color the spaces with G's blue. Color the spaces with H's brown.

F = green   **G** = blue   **H** = brown

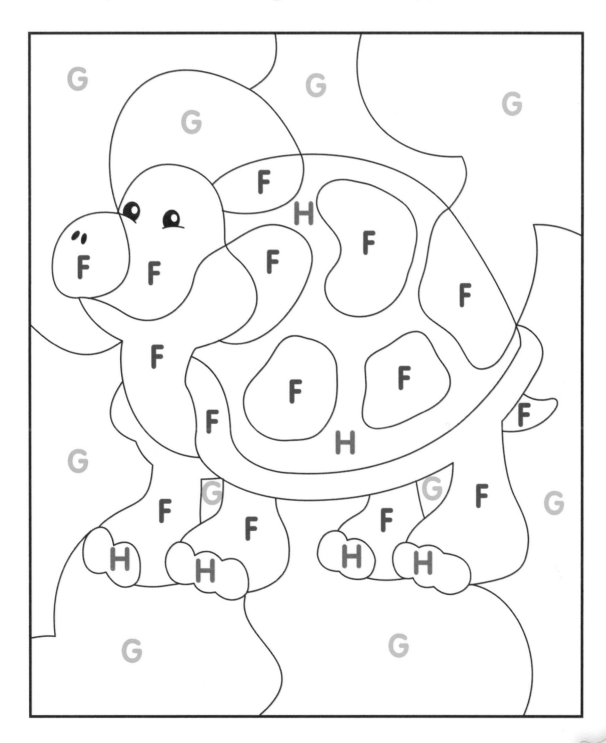

It's FUNdamental! Hidden Pictures

Color the spaces with G's yellow. Color the spaces with H's purple. Color the spaces with I's red.

G = yellow   H = purple   I = red

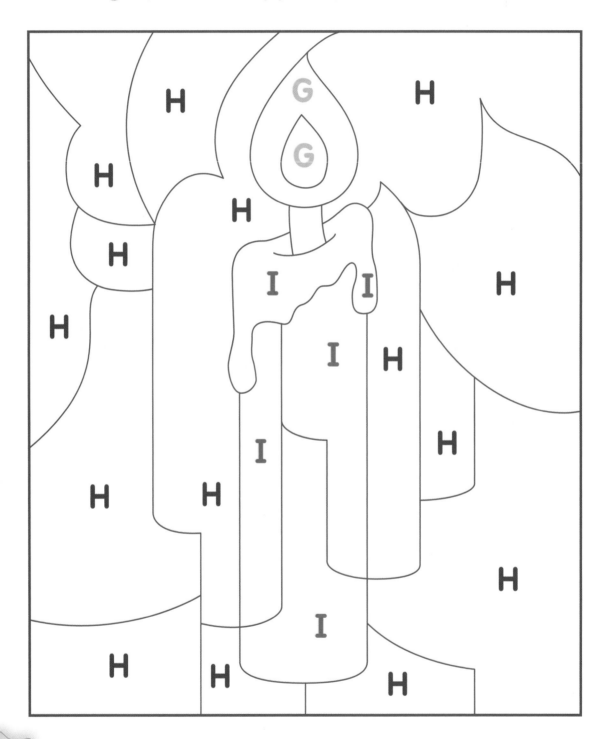

Super Slice

Color to find the hidden picture. Color the spaces with H's red. Color the spaces with I's yellow. Color the spaces with J's brown. Color the spaces with K's blue.

H = red   **I** = yellow   **J** = brown   **K** = blue

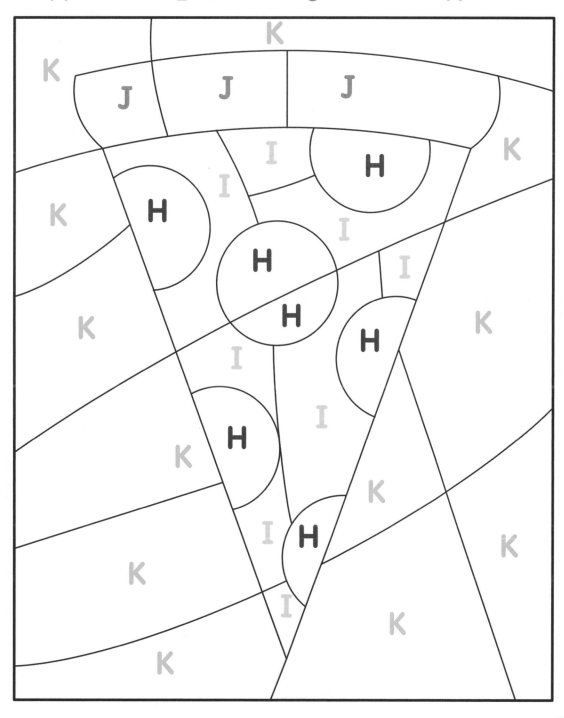

It's FUNdamental! Hidden Pictures

Benny the Bear

Color to find the hidden picture. Color the spaces with I's purple. Color the spaces with J's brown. Color the spaces with K's yellow.

I = purple   **J** = brown   **K** = yellow

Flying High

Color to find the hidden picture. Color the spaces with J's orange. Color the spaces with K's blue. Color the spaces with L's red.

J = orange   K = blue   L = red

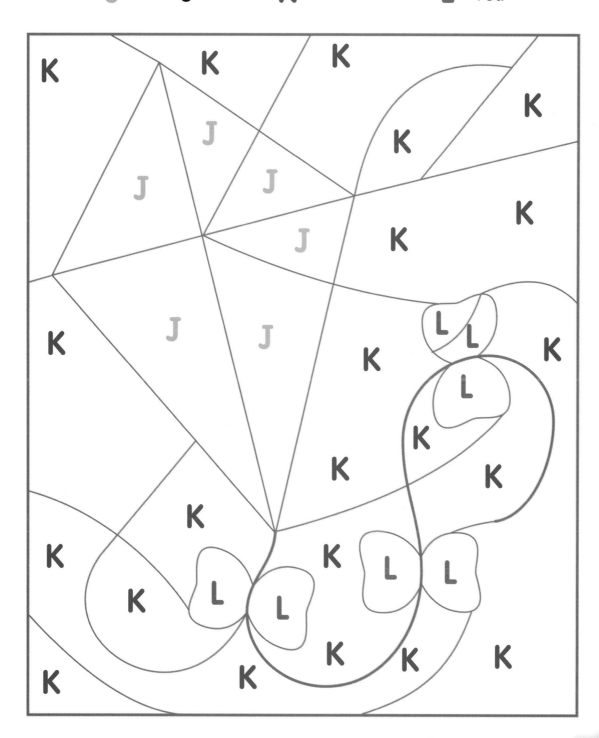

Color to find the hidden picture. Color the spaces with K's blue. Color the spaces with L's green. Color the spaces with M's orange.

K = blue   L = green   M = orange

It's FUNdamental! Hidden Pictures

Wrap It Up

Color to find the hidden picture. Color the spaces with L's purple. Color the spaces with M's green. Color the spaces with N's blue.

L = purple   M = green   N = blue

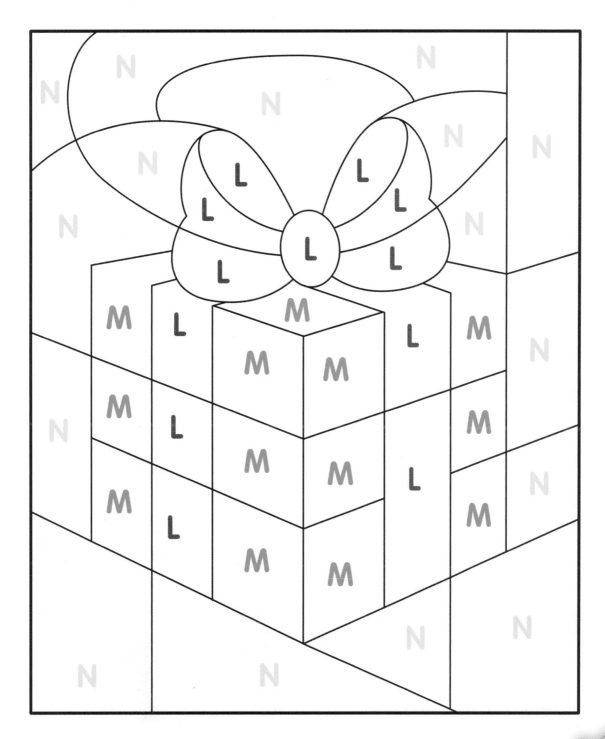

© Rainbow Bridge Publishing

It's FUNdamental! Hidden Pictures

Sammy Scarecrow

Find four triangles in the picture. Circle them.

It's FUNdamental! Hidden Pictures

Find four bananas in the picture. Circle them.

It's FUNdamental! Hidden Pictures

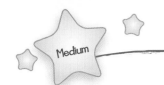
Find these five objects in the picture. Circle them.

It's FUNdamental! Hidden Pictures

Smooth Sailing

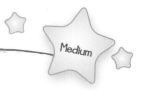

Find these five objects in the picture. Circle them.

It's FUNdamental! Hidden Pictures

Find five bells in the picture. Circle them.

It's FUNdamental! Hidden Pictures

Medium

Find these five objects in the picture. Circle them.

It's FUNdamental! Hidden Pictures

Head of the Class

Find these five objects in the picture. Circle them.

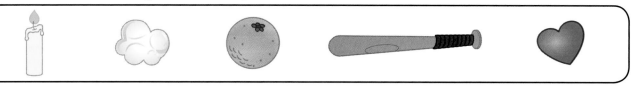

It's FUNdamental! Hidden Pictures

Grocery Shopping

Find these five objects in the picture. Circle them.

It's FUNdamental! Hidden Pictures

Find these six objects in the picture. Circle them.

It's **FUN**damental! Hidden Pictures

Out of This World

Find these six objects in the picture. Circle them.

It's FUNdamental! Hidden Pictures

Piece of Cake

Find these seven objects in the picture. Circle them.

It's FUNdamental! Hidden Pictures

Cactus

Color to find the hidden picture. Color the spaces with diamonds orange.
Color the spaces with rectangles green.

◇ = orange   ▬ = green

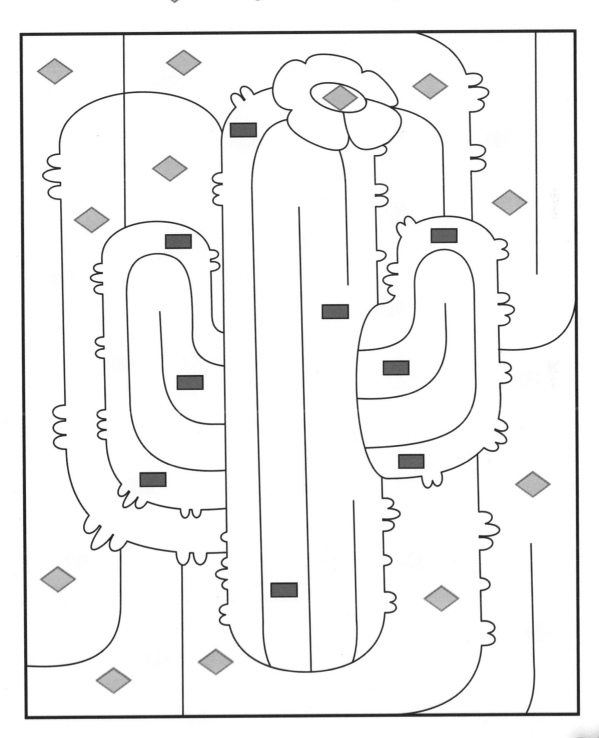

It's FUNdamental! Hidden Pictures

 Medium

Color to find the hidden picture. Color the spaces with ovals blue. Color the spaces with diamonds purple.

⬬ = blue   ◆ = purple

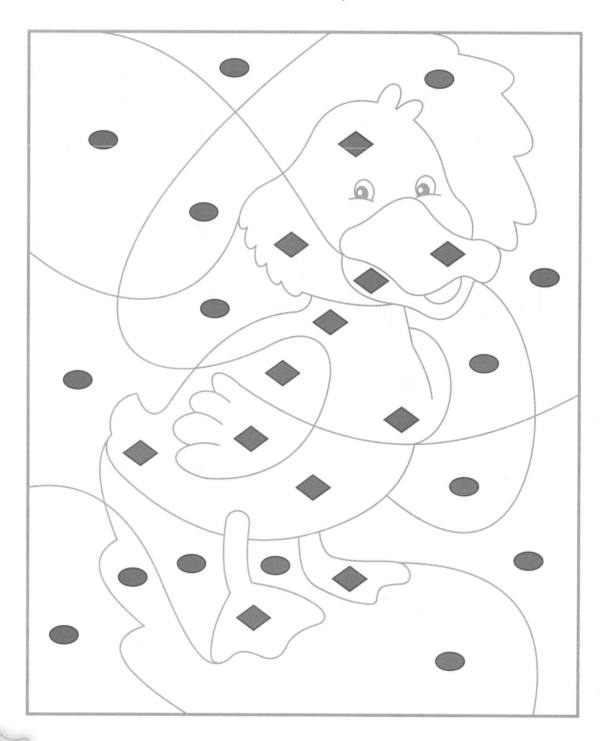

It's FUNdamental! Hidden Pictures

Unlock the Puzzle

Color to find the hidden picture. Color the spaces with diamonds yellow.
Color the spaces with ovals blue.

◆ = yellow   ⬭ = blue

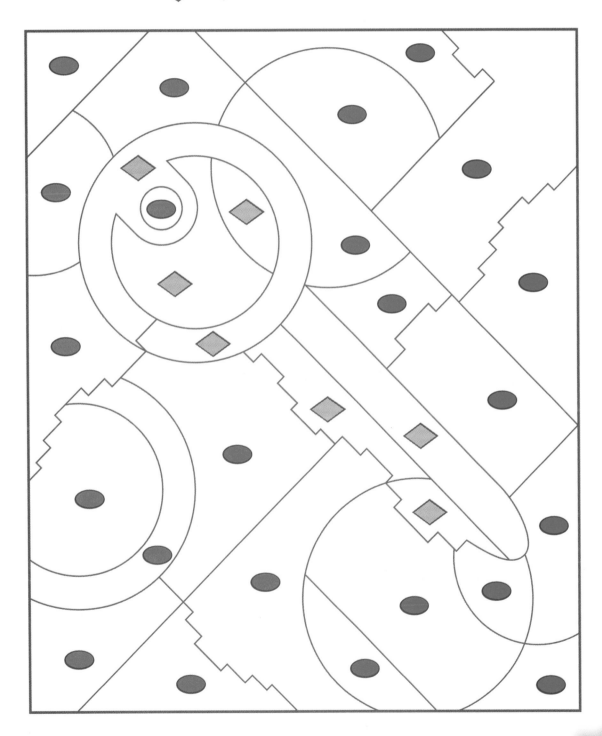

It's FUNdamental! Hidden Pictures

Color to find the hidden picture. Color the spaces with I's green. Color the spaces with 2's blue.

I = green   2 = blue

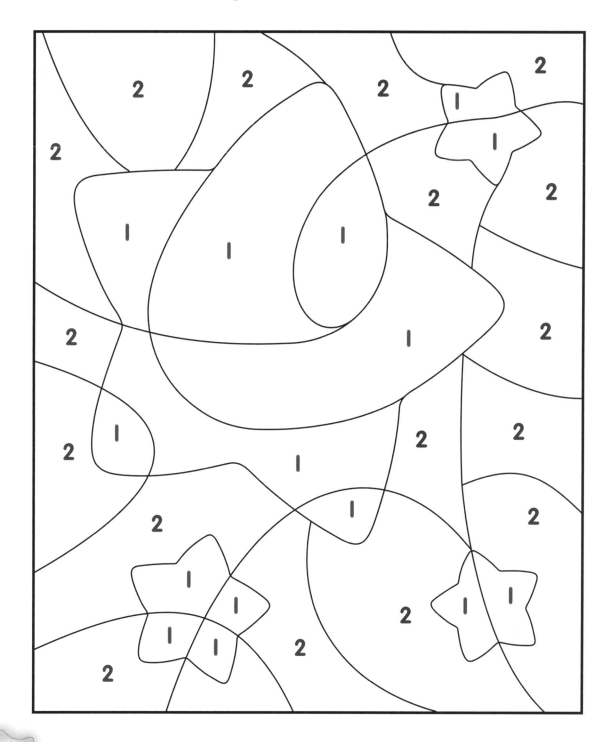

Colorful Crayons

Color to find the hidden picture. Color the spaces with 2's blue. Color the spaces with 3's green.

2 = blue   **3** = green

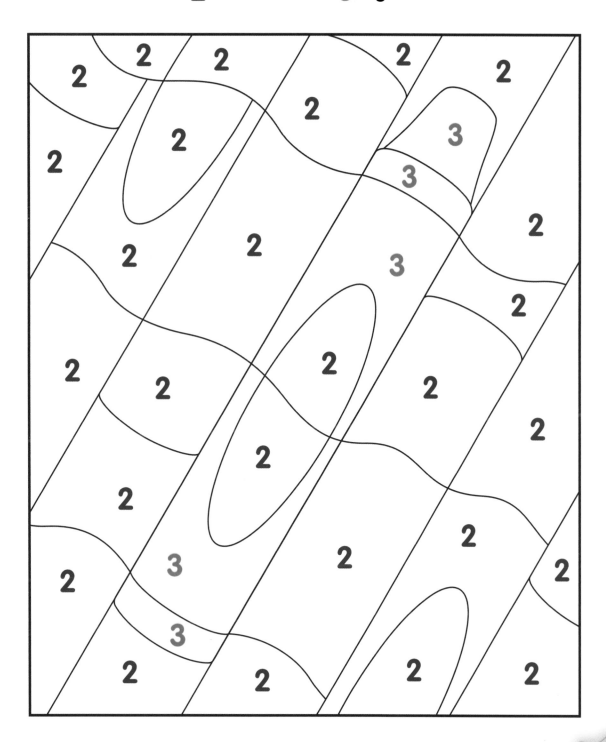

Color to find the hidden picture. Color the spaces with 3's brown. Color the spaces with 4's pink.

3 = brown   **4** = pink

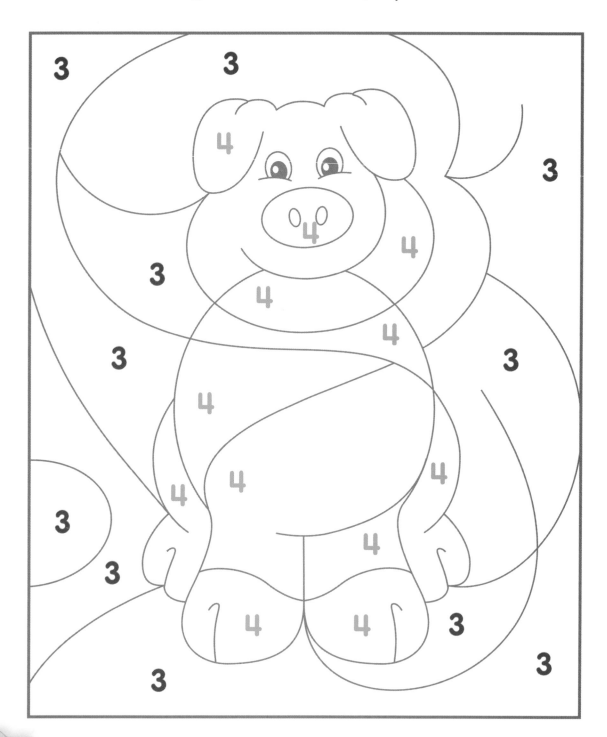

It's FUNdamental! Hidden Pictures

© Rainbow Bridge Publishing

Ring the Bell

Color to find the hidden picture. Color the spaces with 4's yellow. Color the spaces with 5's blue.

4 = yellow   **5** = blue

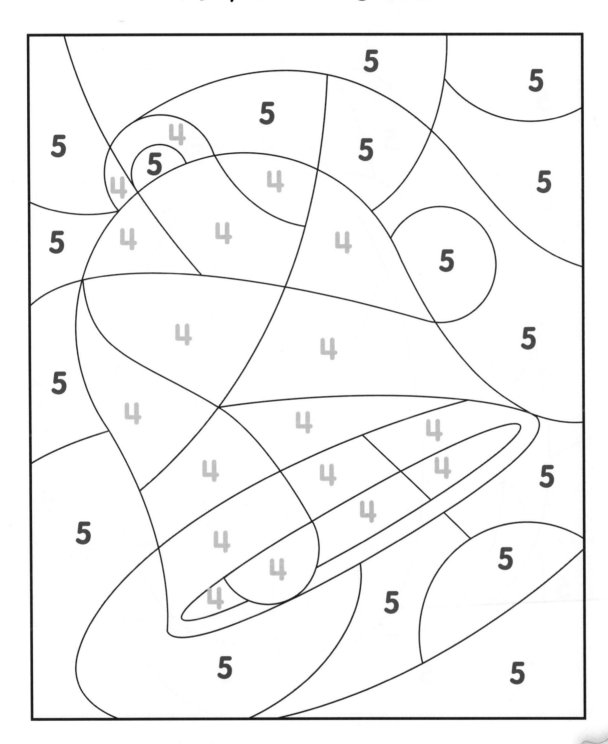

It's FUNdamental! Hidden Pictures

Color to find the hidden picture. Color the spaces with 5's green. Color the spaces with 6's orange.

5 = green   6 = orange

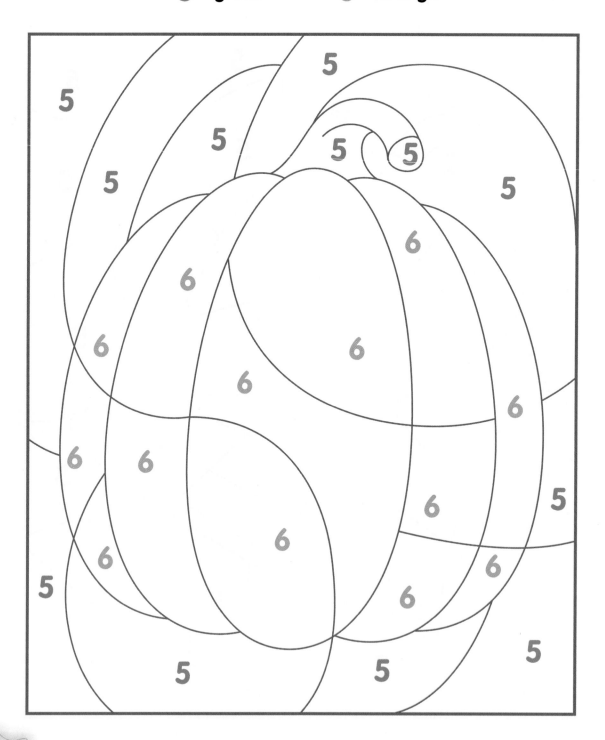

Acorn

Color to find the hidden picture. Color the spaces with 6's brown. Color the spaces with 7's green.

6 = brown   **7** = green

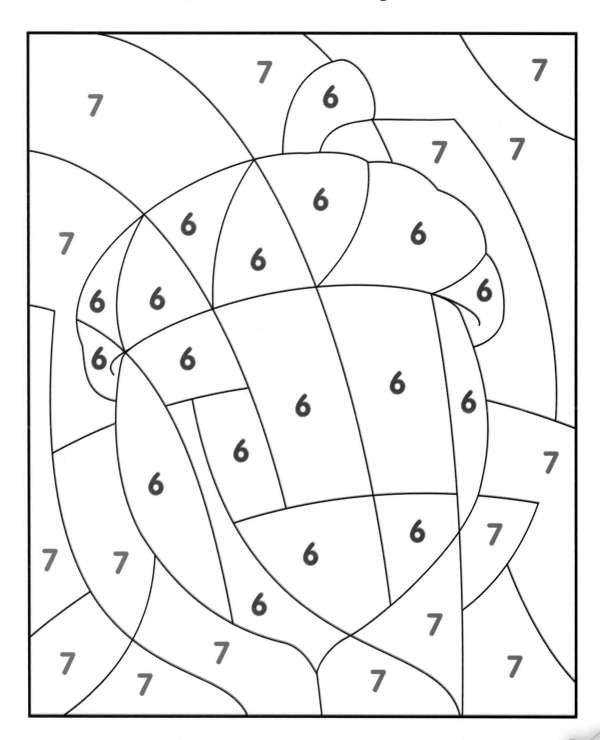

It's FUNdamental! Hidden Pictures

Going Bananas

Color to find the hidden picture. Color the spaces with 7's yellow. Color the spaces with 8's purple.

7 = yellow   **8** = purple

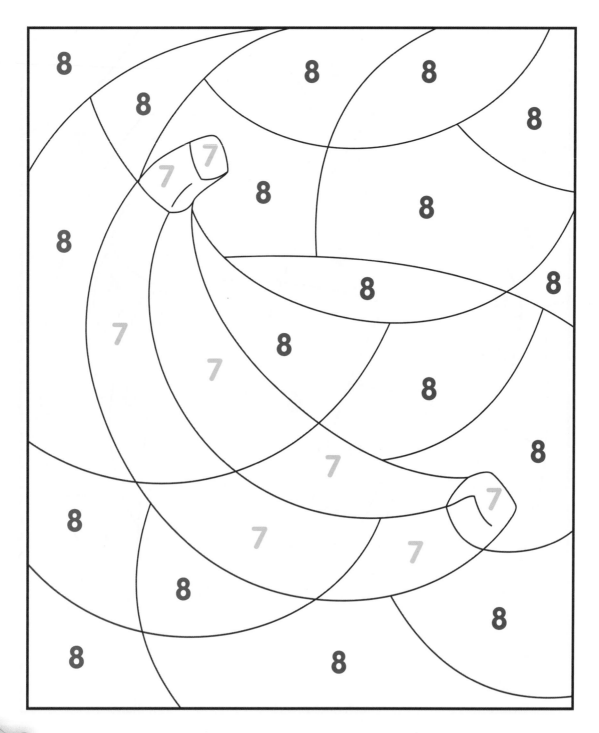

It's FUNdamental! Hidden Pictures

Football Fun

Color to find the hidden picture. Color the spaces with 8's brown. Color the spaces with 9's green.

8 = brown   **9** = green

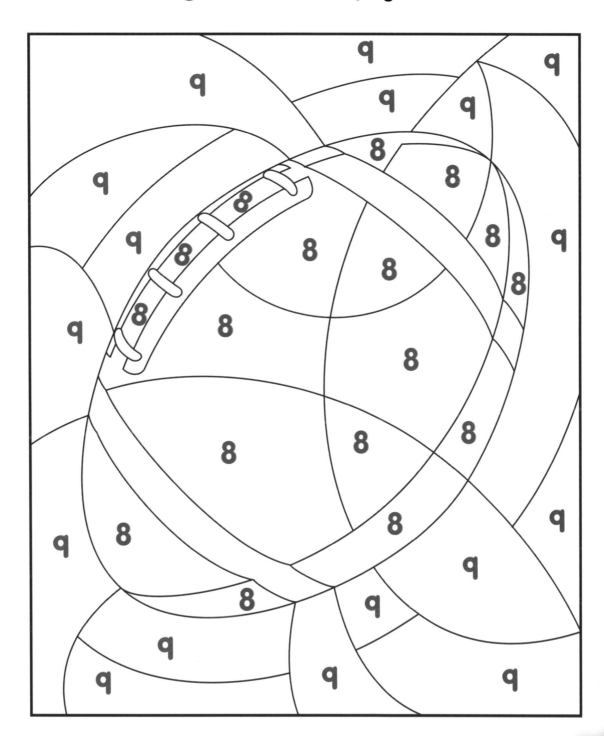

It's FUNdamental! Hidden Pictures

Marvelous Mug

Color to find the hidden picture. Color the spaces with 9's blue. Color the spaces with 10's brown.

9 = blue   10 = brown

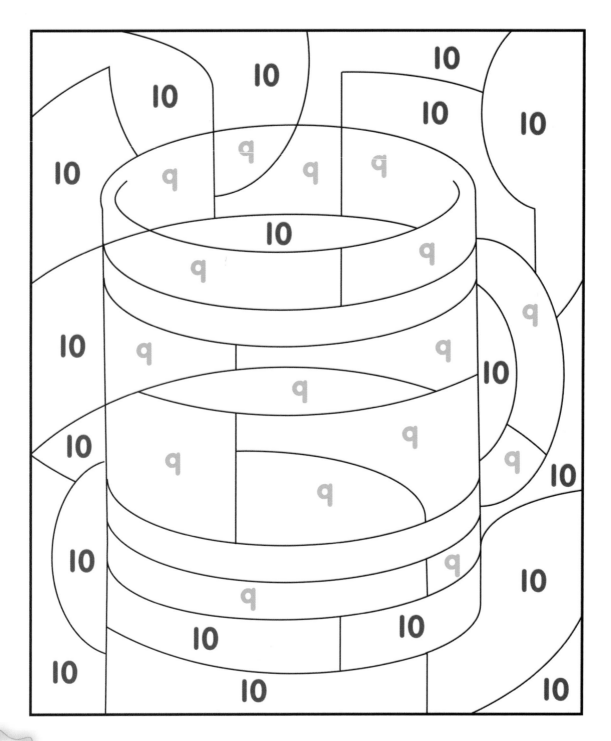

Watermelon

Color to find the hidden picture. Color the spaces with M's green. Color the spaces with N's red. Color the spaces with O's black.

M = green   **N** = red   **O** = black

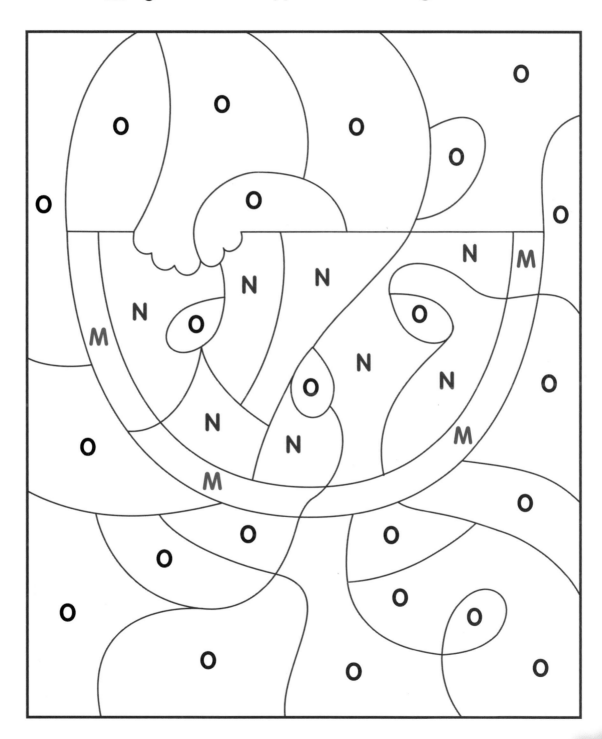

It's FUNdamental! Hidden Pictures

Color to find the hidden picture. Color the spaces with N's orange. Color the spaces with O's red. Color the spaces with P's green.

N = orange   **O** = red   **P** = green

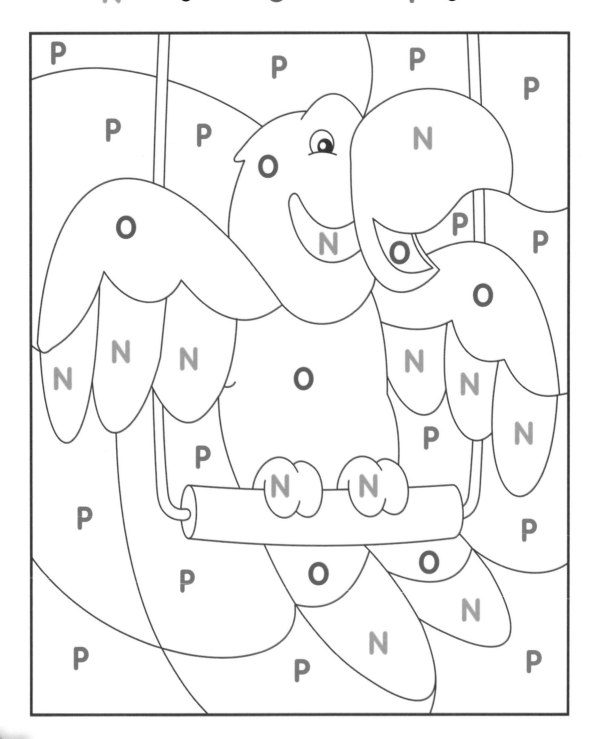

It's FUNdamental! Hidden Pictures

All Wrapped Up

Color to find the hidden picture. Color the spaces with O's red. Color the spaces with P's blue. Color the spaces with Q's gray.

O = red   **P** = blue   **Q** = gray

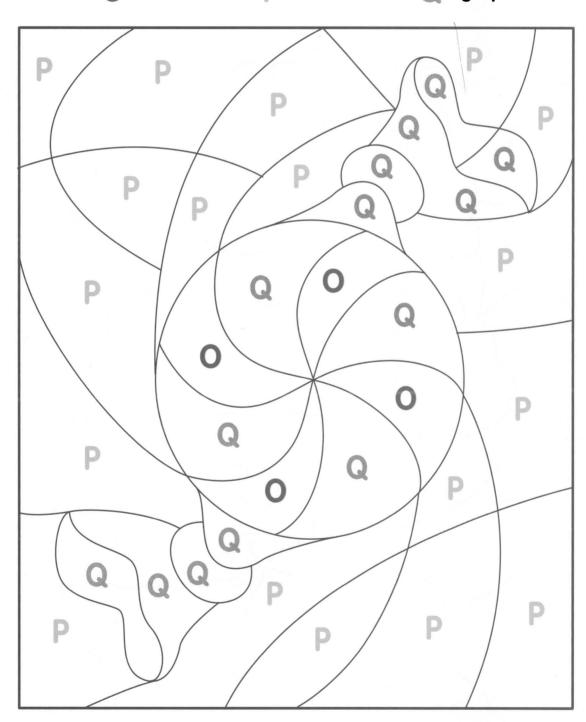

It's FUNdamental! Hidden Pictures

Ice Cream Sundae

Color to find the hidden picture. Color the spaces with P's red. Color the spaces with Q's blue. Color the spaces with R's brown.

P = red   **Q** = blue   **R** = brown

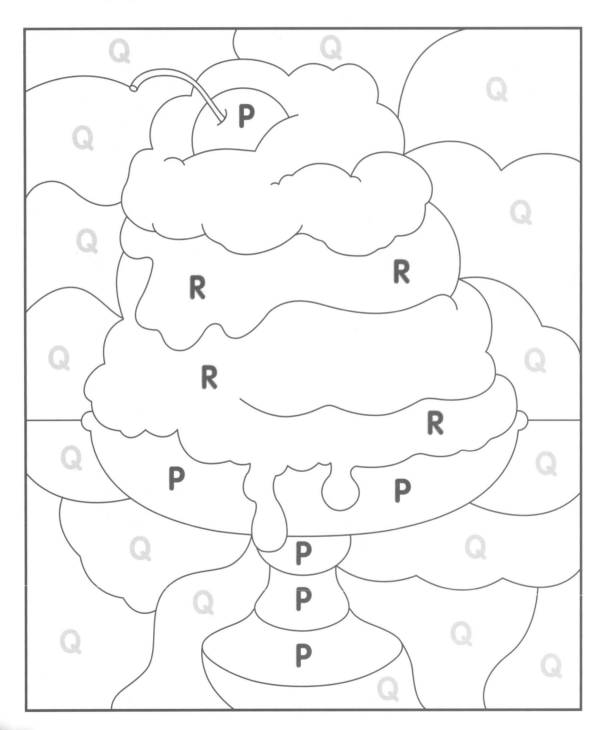

Space Adventure

Color to find the hidden picture. Color the spaces with Q's blue. Color the spaces with R's gold. Color the spaces with S's red.

Q = blue   R = gold   S = red

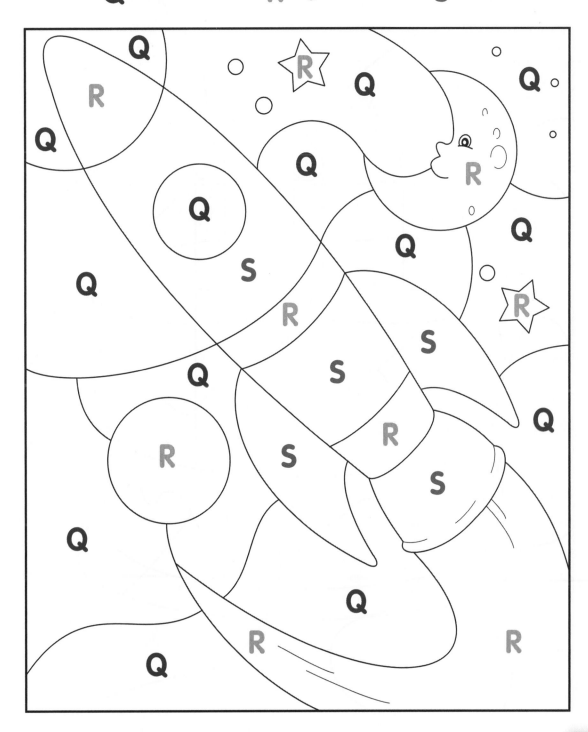

© Rainbow Bridge Publishing   It's FUNdamental! Hidden Pictures

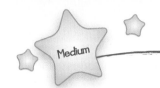
Color to find the hidden picture. Color the spaces with R's red. Color the spaces with S's orange. Color the spaces with T's blue.

R = red   **S** = orange   T = blue

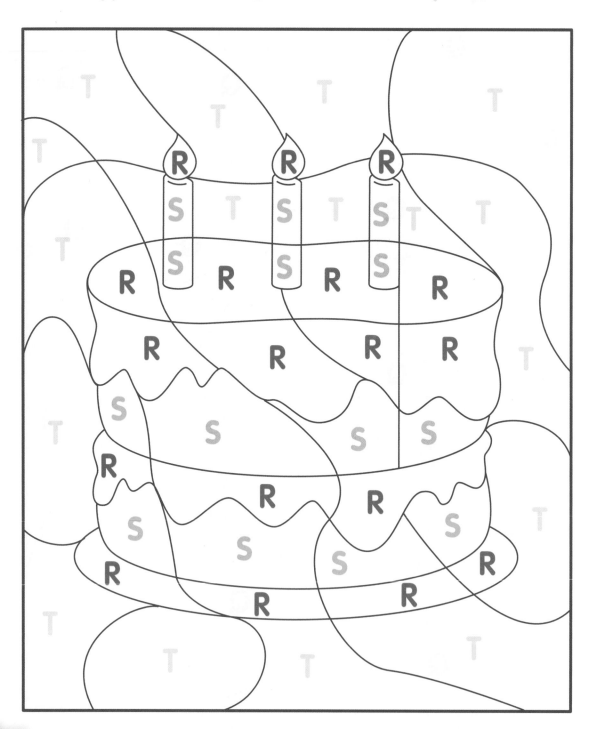

An Apple a Day

Medium

Color to find the hidden picture. Color the spaces with S's purple. Color the spaces with T's green. Color the spaces with U's red.

S = purple   **T** = green   **U** = red

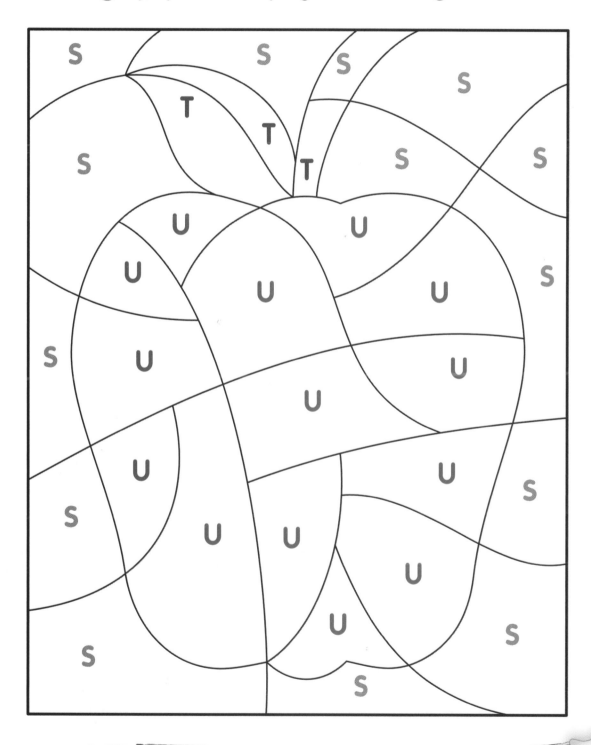

Little Dinosaur

Color to find the hidden picture. Color the spaces with T's purple. Color the spaces with U's green. Color the spaces with V's blue.

T = purple   U = green   V = blue

It's FUNdamental! Hidden Pictures

© Rainbow Bridge Publishing

Riding the Bus

Color to find the hidden picture. Color the spaces with U's gray. Color the spaces with V's orange. Color the spaces with W's green.

U = gray   V = orange   W = green

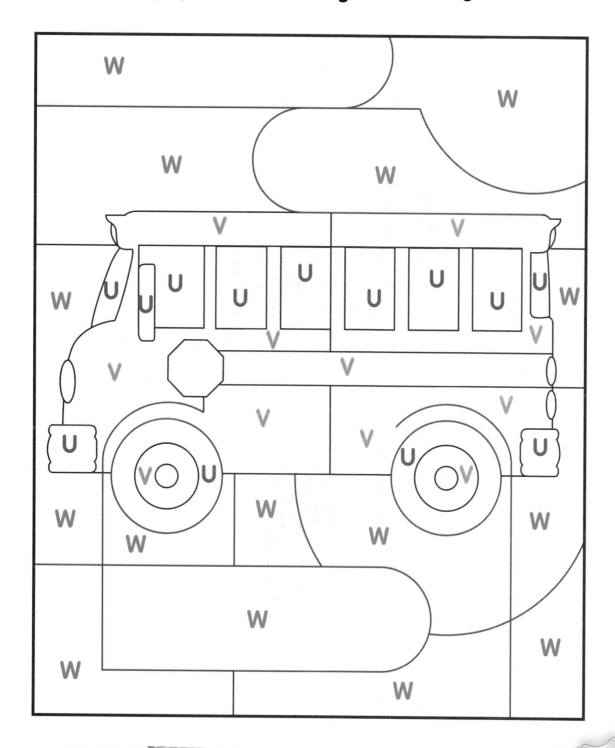

Best of the Bunch

Color to find the hidden picture. Color the spaces with V's green. Color the spaces with W's purple. Color the spaces with X's yellow.

V = green   **W** = purple   **X** = yellow

It's FUNdamental! Hidden Pictures

Seashell

Color to find the hidden picture. Color the spaces with W's blue. Color the spaces with X's pink. Color the spaces with Y's purple.

W = blue   **X** = pink   **Y** = purple

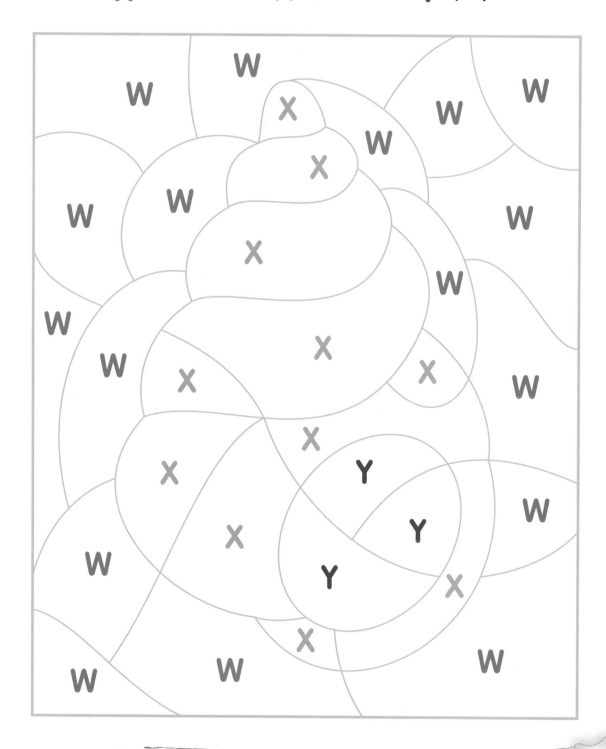

Color to find the hidden picture. Color the spaces with X's purple. Color the spaces with Y's yellow. Color the spaces with Z's pink.

X = purple   Y = yellow   Z = pink

It's FUNdamental! Hidden Pictures

Big Cheese

Find these eight objects in the picture. Circle them.

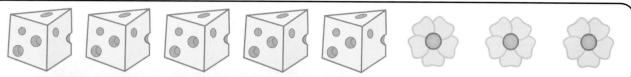

It's FUNdamental! Hidden Pictures

Hard

Find these eight objects in the picture. Circle them.

Wild Animals

It's FUNdamental! Hidden Pictures

Cool Classroom

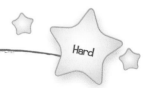

Find these eight objects in the picture. Circle them.

It's FUNdamental! Hidden Pictures

Find these eight objects in the picture. Circle them.

It's FUNdamental! Hidden Pictures

Sea Scene

Find these eight objects in the picture. Circle them.

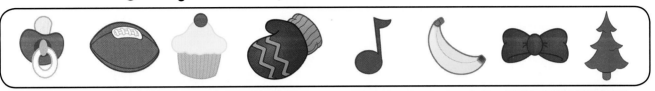

It's FUNdamental! Hidden Pictures

Curious Camper

Find these nine objects in the picture. Circle them.

It's FUNdamental! Hidden Pictures

© Rainbow Bridge Publishing

Library Fun

Find nine crayons in the picture. Circle them.

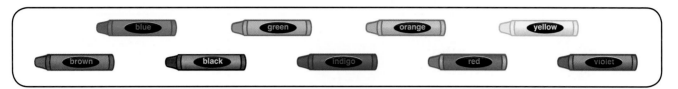

Clarence the Clown

Find these nine objects in the picture. Circle them.

It's FUNdamental! Hidden Pictures

Winter Wonder

Find these nine objects in the picture. Circle them.

It's FUNdamental! Hidden Pictures

Happy Bird

Find these 10 objects in the picture. Circle them.

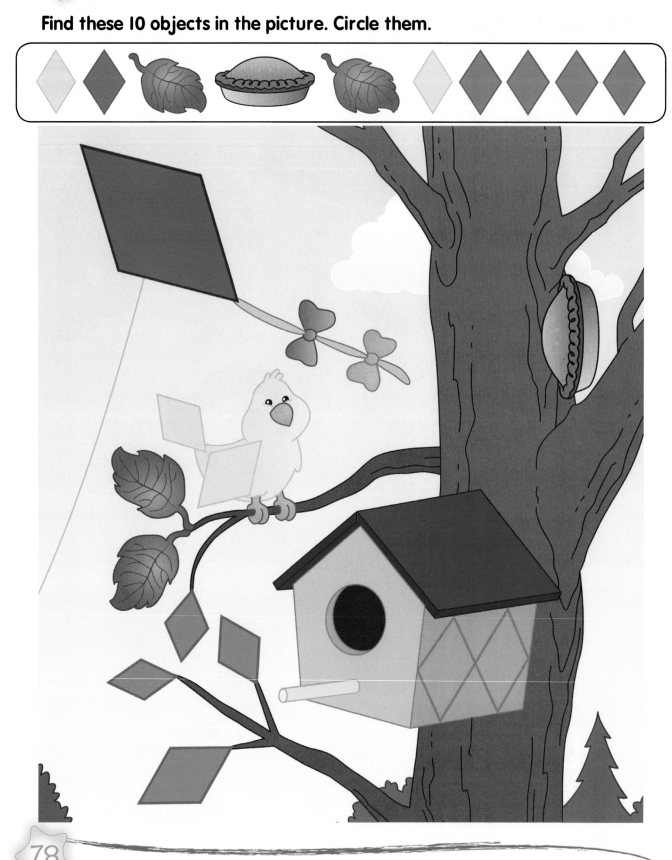

Scrub-a-Dub

Find these 10 fish in the picture. Circle them.

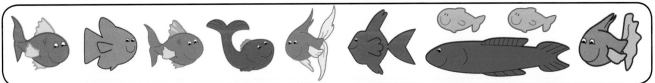

It's FUNdamental! Hidden Pictures

Sue's Sand Castle

Find the numbers 0–5 in the picture. Circle them.

0 1 2 3 4 5

© Rainbow Bridge Publishing

Jill's Garden

Find the numbers 6–10 in the picture. Circle them.

6 7 8 9 10

It's **FUN**damental! Hidden Pictures

Find the numbers 1–9 in the picture. Circle them.

1 2 3 4 5 6 7 8 9

It's FUNdamental! Hidden Pictures

A Day at the Beach

Find the numbers 0–10 in the picture. Circle them.

| 0 | 1 | 2 | 3 | 4 | 5 | 6 | 7 | 8 | 9 | 10 |

It's FUNdamental! Hidden Pictures

Lots of Light

Color to find the hidden picture. Color the spaces with a's yellow. Color the spaces with b's red. Color the spaces with c's green. Color the spaces with d's blue.

a = yellow   b = red   c = green   d = blue

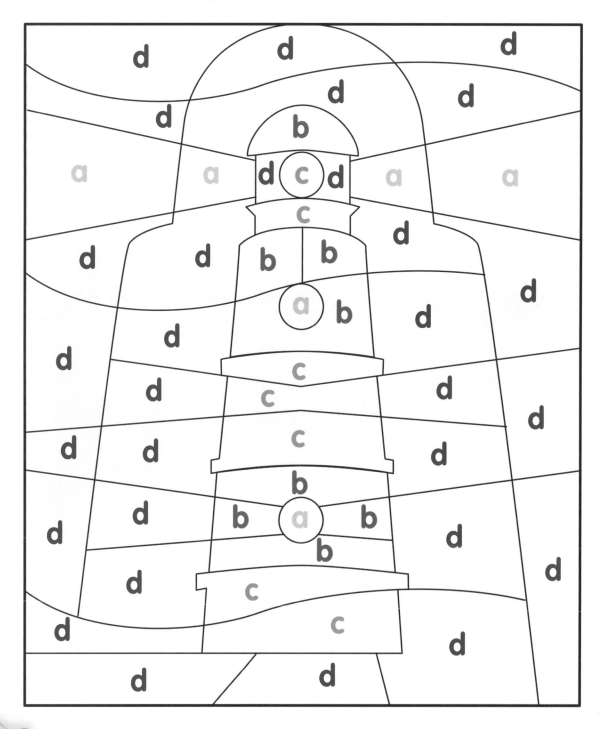

It's FUNdamental! Hidden Pictures

Up, Up, and Away

Color to find the hidden picture. Color the spaces with c's blue. Color the spaces with d's green. Color the spaces with e's red. Color the spaces with f's light blue.

c = blue   **d** = green   **e** = red   f = light blue

It's FUNdamental! Hidden Pictures

Hard

Color to find the hidden picture. Color the spaces with e's blue. Color the spaces with f's red. Color the spaces with g's yellow. Color the spaces with h's green.

e = blue   f = red   g = yellow   h = green

It's FUNdamental! Hidden Pictures

Simon Snail

Color to find the hidden picture. Color the spaces with g's gold. Color the spaces with h's green. Color the spaces with i's orange. Color the spaces with j's blue.

g = gold   **h** = green   **i** = orange   **j** = blue

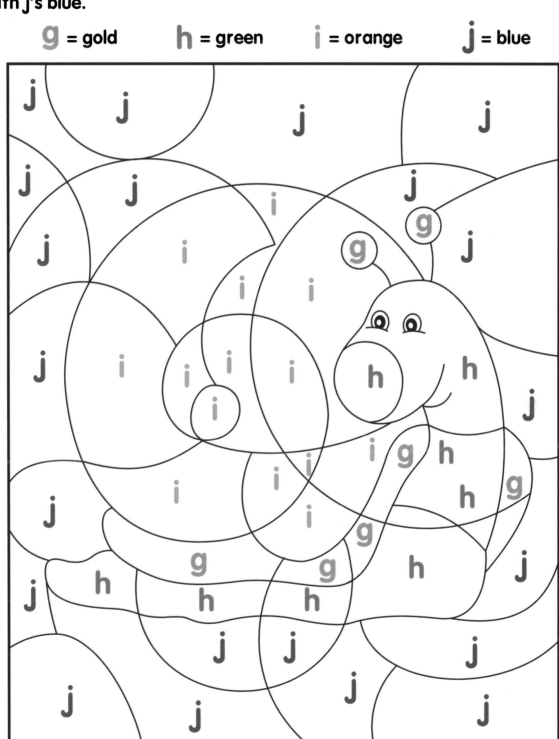

It's FUNdamental! Hidden Pictures

Color to find the hidden picture. Color the spaces with i's red. Color the spaces with j's blue. Color the spaces with k's pink. Color the spaces with l's green.

i = red   j = blue   k = pink   l = green

It's FUNdamental! Hidden Pictures   © Rainbow Bridge Publishing

Cupcake

Color to find the hidden picture. Color the spaces with k's gold. Color the spaces with l's pink. Color the spaces with m's green. Color the spaces with n's red.

k = gold   l = pink   m = green   n = red

© Rainbow Bridge Publishing   It's FUNdamental! Hidden Pictures

Color to find the hidden picture. Color the spaces with m's blue. Color the spaces with n's orange. Color the spaces with o's red. Color the spaces with p's green.

m = blue   n = orange   o = red   p = green

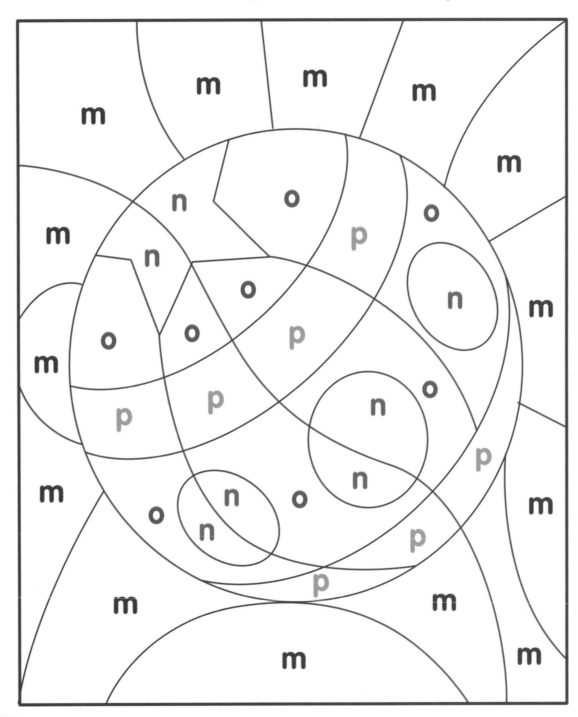

Dandy Drum

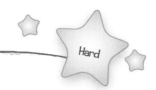

Color to find the hidden picture. Color the spaces with o's blue. Color the spaces with p's red. Color the spaces with q's orange. Color the spaces with r's green.

o = blue   p = red   q = orange   r = green

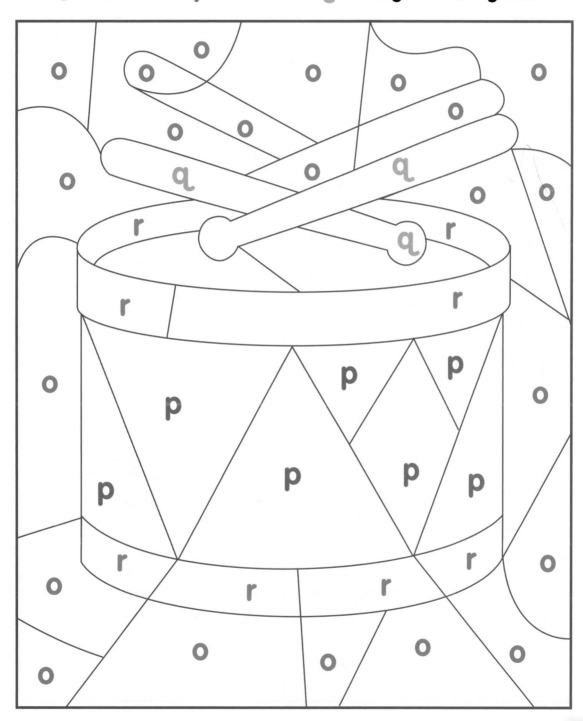

It's FUNdamental! Hidden Pictures

Color to find the hidden picture. Color the spaces with q's red. Color the spaces with r's blue. Color the spaces with s's silver. Color the spaces with t's green.

q = red   r = blue   s = silver   t = green

It's FUNdamental! Hidden Pictures

© Rainbow Bridge Publishing

Betsy Butterfly

Color to find the hidden picture. Color the spaces with s's purple. Color the spaces with t's green. Color the spaces with u's yellow. Color the spaces with v's pink.

S = purple   **t** = green   **U** = yellow   **V** = pink

It's **FUN**damental! Hidden Pictures

Cheery Cardinal

Color to find the hidden picture. Color the spaces with u's blue. Color the spaces with v's brown. Color the spaces with w's red. Color the spaces with x's gold.

U = blue   **V** = brown   **W** = red   **X** = gold

It's FUNdamental! Hidden Pictures

© Rainbow Bridge Publishing

Gumball Machine

Color to find the hidden picture. Color the spaces with w's green. Color the spaces with x's red. Color the spaces with y's purple. Color the spaces with z's pink.

W = green   X = red   Y = purple   Z = pink

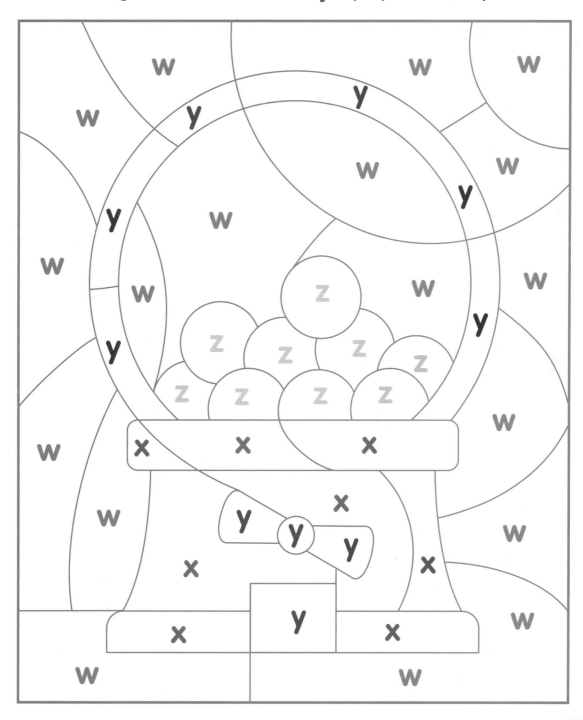

It's FUNdamental! Hidden Pictures

Hard

Find the letters A–Z in the picture. Circle them.

A B C **D** E F G H I **J** K L M
N O P Q R S T U V **W** X **Y** Z

It's FUNdamental! Hidden Pictures